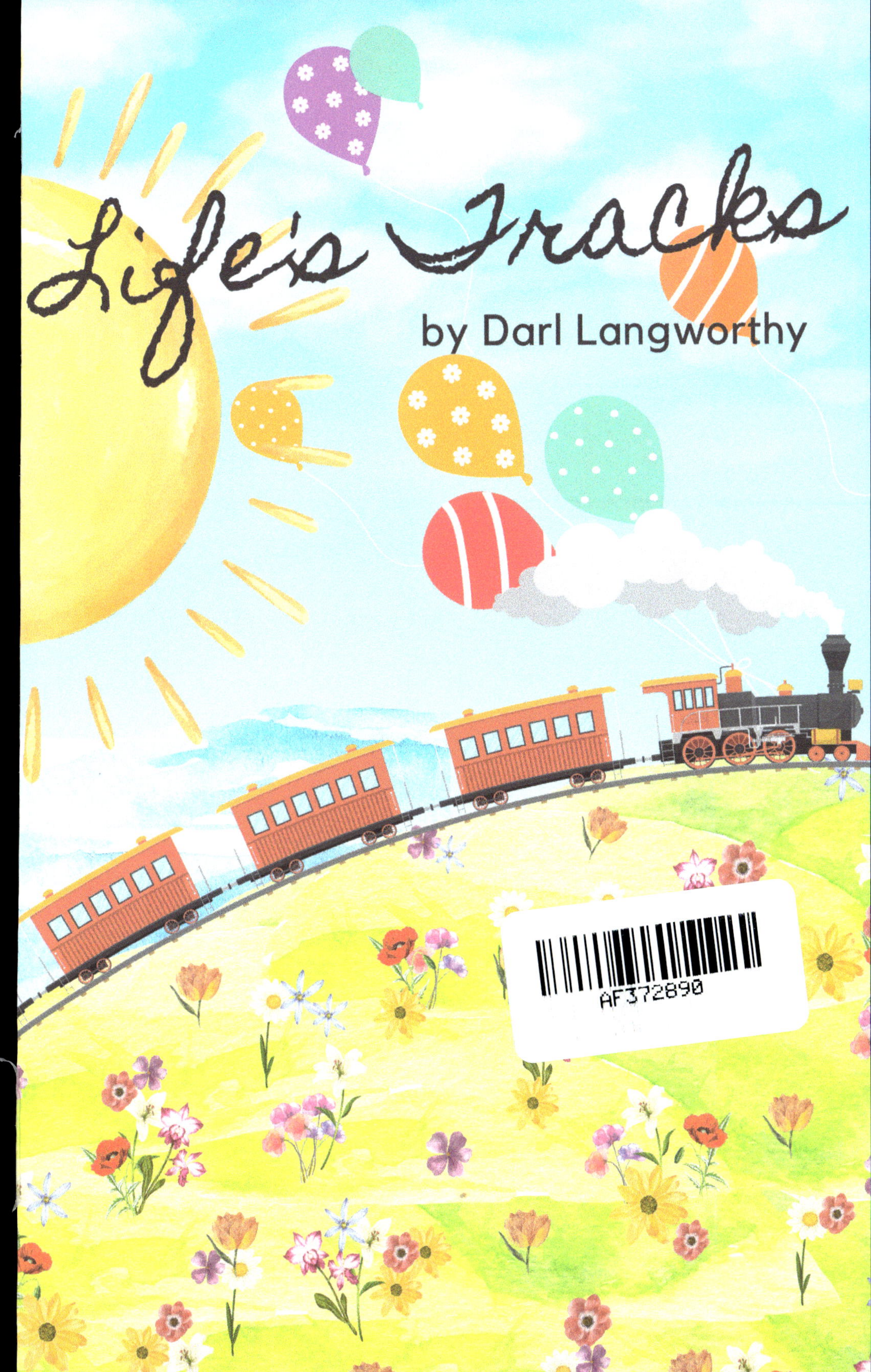
Life's Tracks
by Darl Langworthy

ISBN 979-8-89043-635-1 (paperback)
ISBN 979-8-89043-636-8 (digital)

Christian Faith Publishing
832 Park Avenue
Meadville, PA 16335
www.christianfaithpublishing.com

Printed in the United States of America

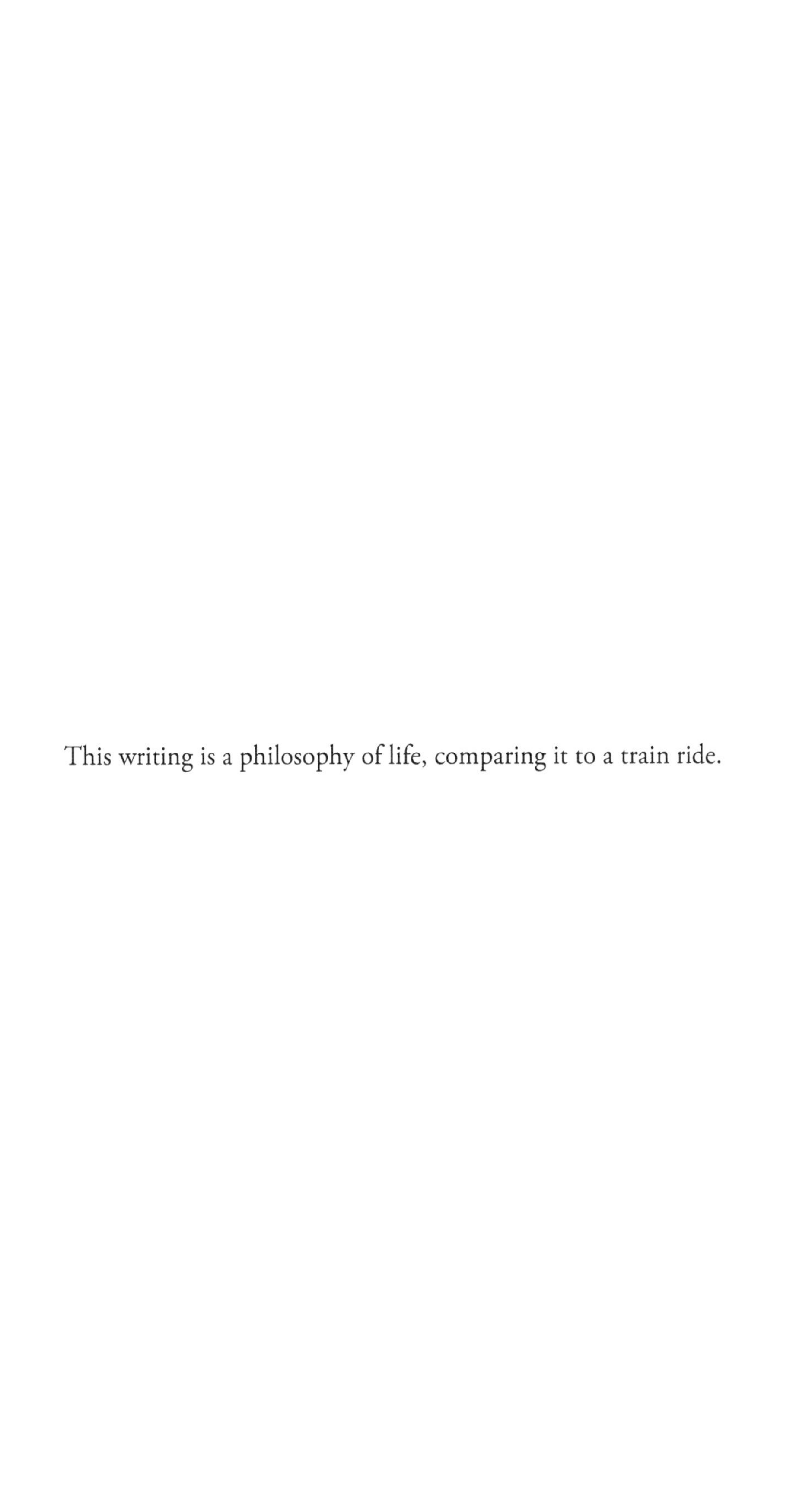
This writing is a philosophy of life, comparing it to a train ride.

Dedication

This book is my contribution to the world so that I may finish my journey knowing I gave back.

Preface

We are all waiting to get on the train of life. Get your ticket early through faith and belief. Don't stand in line too long or with too much baggage. Don't place importance on things that will only bog you down, such as youth, money, and self-importance.

Learn to stand in line and be patient. Move forward when it's your turn to get aboard the train. Many detours arise, but don't get distracted. Keep riding and learning about Jesus and heaven. As you journey along, grow in your faith, and help others to grow in theirs.

Take a ride through whatever generation you are in. Let your light shine! Success in life depends on the talents you have been given and how you use those talents. We are all waiting for our ticket to heaven's eternity, but we have many stops before our destination.

Contents

Youthful Journey

When I was young, I held my mother's hand and waited for my dad to come back with our tickets. We were going to see my grandparents in another state. When we arrived, I remembered the smells and sights of youth. The excitement childhood brings in enjoying simple delights at my grandparents' house, like the smell of pancakes, cookies, and pies. And, oh yes, the flowers!

Their sparkling eyes and voices bring soft loving caresses and hugs to last for months. Grandma's words of affirmation, like "Bless your heart" or strong words of advice from grandpa, such as "Don't bite your fingernails or else you'll end up with a ball of nails in your stomach that you can't digest." The innocence of childhood, thinking your parents or grandparents can do no wrong.

A Ride of a Lifetime

Then life drops you off to mature years when you find out new discoveries. The reality of being a teenager and feeling warm, fuzzy feelings about many things. Things like our own bodies and other young women and men, and enjoying movies about family and Christmas, just the overall sense of love and joy that different seasons bring, becoming spiritual and knowing there is a God that you want to live for and love always.

Other discoveries, such as listening to music and experiencing deep emotions that erupt inside of me. The fascination with movie stars and wanting fame and fortune, only to find out later the lure of it all is a falsehood or perhaps the longing to be on stage and applauded with a standing ovation, not realizing that God is always applauding us on his stage.

Asking questions on the mysteries of life, unexplained questions of feelings and thoughts, sharing special moments with brothers and sisters, realizing that even though we are siblings, we are different in our own ways and grasp our individuality. Seeing the train of life take family members far, far away, into new and perhaps painful lives full of lessons and regrets. Understanding that when we leave home, we will not return the same. The train knows this truth.

Middle Years

The middle years come, and we're forced to learn to survive on our own as we watch our parents grow older and our grandparents reach their final ride, knowing they were good people and feeling happy they are in eternity. Even though we hoped it would be, the final resting place doesn't feel the same for everyone.

Raising our own children with unconditional love for each, helping them understand and navigate this life through all of its struggles, teaching them the power of endurance while showing patience to love and to be loved, not pushing our own expectations on to our children, but allowing them to seek their own desires, allowing ourselves to let go and let them navigate this life in their own way while remembering to set aside our judgment, and instead, push them with love and acceptance.

Our children, like our siblings, are all different individuals. If only we were given a manual on how to raise them; but we must learn as we go and accept the mistakes and victories that come with parenthood. Remember, it's the journey that prepares you for the destination.

Senior Years

We then ride along to become grandparents ourselves. We look back at our mistakes and successes and hope to help our children, and now grandchildren, learn from them. We've gained an understanding of humility by helping others, not being full of pride, but remembering to give in return for joy.

Don't take yourself too seriously during these years. Laugh and be happy. Protect your mind, and don't let spiritual warfare enter. Put on the armor of God, and protect yourself from unworthy thoughts. Do not be distracted by obstacles or detours, but stay on course, knowing that they were really just opportunities in disguise.

Train tickets of life are expensive. We must earn our own ride. Some get their tickets early, and it takes others forever. In the end, we all get the same opportunities, but we are not all given the same knowledge.

We learn that we never graduate from the gospel of life, but we do increase our spirituality throughout our journey. By practicing his presence every day, we realize how real he is. And although we all have an expiration date, we must ask ourselves if we've done all we should have so that we may arrive at the end without regrets.

Truths

We get our strength and acceptance from God, not anyone else. Choose the direction of your train correctly. We trust the train to stay on track. God keeps us on course and embraces us for our final ride into his arms.

Don't believe the many lies that come your way. We must learn discipline as temptations abound. Take the time to learn real truths on questions about your journey. And as we come closer to our final ride, we must make the necessary adjustments. We should never take our eyes off the goal of life. Don't let the detours trip us, but continue to learn as we ride the train. Trust in the Lord as we journey through life.

Notice the wonders of God's creation and pay attention to how it affects us. We are taught to be grace given, not fear driven. Grace is a free favor from God because he loves us, regardless of our actions. As we journey, pause, at times, and be still; solitude can be uplifting and good for the soul.

Meaningful Experiences

Don't make our children perform from fear. Teach them the value of commitment. We are all learning to respond, not react. Commit to excellence.

We should remember, as we grow old, that our children are also growing and struggling. It seems, at times, they have forgotten about us, but they haven't. They are so overwhelmed with life that they don't realize we are sad, not knowing them anymore.

Learn to love yourself! And then it becomes easier to love others. Focus on changing yourself before trying to change everyone else. Oh, what a beautiful ride we're on when we keep our eyes open to the wonder of commitment to excellence in the journey of life.

Final Ride

We have to go through valleys before we arrive at the highest destination. The Lord works in the middle of our messes. We must praise him during this time. Don't wait for storms to pass, but dance in the midst of the rain, for rain and wind will come into all of our lives, but God is the only thing that can fill our hearts entirely. Pray together, play together, and never forget to have fun. A smile will take you far!

I have experienced hardships and have witnessed miracles. Knowing these experiences, I've realized the joyful greatness ahead. Save your resources for life's final ride into eternity—the loving arms of God. The rewards are immense!

Copyedited and Illustrated by Ellen McAfee

www.ingramcontent.com/pod-product-compliance
Lightning Source LLC
Chambersburg PA
CBHW040120150726
48005CB00013B/1800